Spring Flowe

G000122701

MARK J. WESTON

Flower arrangements by Jane Weston

Photography by Roger Tuff   Artwork by Ian G. Wheeler

Printed in Great Britain by
Millbrook Press, Totton, Southampton

© MARK J. WESTON

SBN 901131 03 2

FOUR SEASONS PUBLICATIONS
The Stables, Monxton, Nr. Andover, Hants, SP11 8AT.

PREFACE

The fresh green new spring flowers present their particular seasonal challenge to the flower arranger. As flowers become plentiful, more elaborate arrangements can be envisaged, and the skill of the arranger is tested to the full.

Knowledge of the basic flower arranging techniques is essential if full advantage is to be made of the wide range of flowers available, and study of this book and its three seasonal companion volumes should pay substantial dividends.

In the past most flower arrangers have tended to be self-taught and even the most experienced may well find time well spent in a quick study of the basic methods.

In any event the receipt of hundreds of letters from people who have studied this flower arranging series indicate clearly that the methods detailed are very effective and that proficiency can be substantially improved over a short period.

I hope that you will find this book and the others useful and good value, and that your enjoyment from flowers and flower arranging continues to expand.

MARK J. WESTON

CONTENTS

"Oasis"

Pinholders

Chicken Wire & Scissors

EQUIPMENT

"Oasis" is a water absorbent plastic foam which is available from your flower shop in several shapes and sizes. Flower stems inserted into "Oasis" are held firmly in position. It should be well soaked in water before use and can be cut with a table knife to the required size. After the flowers have been arranged it is important to keep the "Oasis" continually moist by adding water. When the flowers are finally spent the "Oasis" can be used for subsequent arrangements. There are other plastic foam mounts available such as "Florapak" "Stemfix" and "Savannah" but "Oasis" has been used for all the arrangements in this book.

Pinholders in many shapes and sizes are available from your flower shop. They are a useful substitute for "Oasis" particularly when line arrangements in shallow dishes are required. They can also be used in conjunction with "Oasis" or wire-netting (see below).

Chicken Wire. 2" chicken wire-netting is also an inexpensive flower arranging medium. It would be cut from the roll and crumpled up before insertion into the container.

Scissors. When arranging flowers it is most desirable to use a pair of special

Sprayer

flower scissors. These have one blade with a serrated edge designed to stop the scissors from slipping on the flower stem. They are readily available from your flower shop.

Sprayer. An atomizer spray is very useful for spraying arrangements with water after completion. The tiny water droplets help to keep the flowers and foliage in fresh condition.

CONTAINERS

The choice of flowers for a particular style of arrangement governs the selection of the container. It is important that there should be compatibility in this respect. In this book thirteen different containers have been used for the seventeen arrangements involved and they should all be inexpensively available from your flower shop.

Small plastic urn. An inexpensive container suitable for petite arrangements.

Large plastic bowl. An ordinary inexpensive bowl suitable for all-the-way-round and triangular arrangements.

Hamper. The round lid of this basket acts as a backcloth to crescent, diagonal and asymmetrical arrangements.

Boat-shaped basket. In common with other baskets a metal lining is required. The handle will play a complementary role in conjunction with crescent and L-shaped arrangements.

Oblong trough. Being a rough pottery container it is inexpensive and most suitable for line arrangements using simple flowers.

Square trough. Requiring either "Oasis" or wire netting this trough is very versatile

Small plastic urn   Large plastic bowl

Hamper

Oblong trough   Square trough

Boat-shaped basket

Posy ring   Copper jug

Rectangular basket

Rectangular basket with handle   Shallow dish

Posy ring. Suitable not only as a container for very short flower heads (left over from a larger arrangement) but also for orthodox decorations when used in conjunction with an "Oasis" block.

Copper jug. The curves of handle and lip make this particularly suitable for asymmetrical arrangements.

Rectangular basket. Lacking curves this basket is more suitable for the triangular and L-shaped arrangements.

Rectangular basket with handle. Having a metal lining filled with "Oasis" the triangular and all-the-way-round arrangements are the most fitting.

Shallow dish. With pinholder or "Oasis" this simple dish becomes extremely versatile.

Rectangular trough. In conjunction with pinholder or "Oasis" this shape is most suitable for diagonal or line arrangements.

Rectangular trough   "Oasis" container

"Oasis" container. Available in plastic and pottery and in several sizes, this inexpensive container takes a cylinder of "Oasis" making it very versatile.

WIRING FLOWERS

After a flower has been wired the stem can be moulded to the required shape which will then be retained. The wire also acts as a support when used with limp or thin stemmed flowers.

1. A 22° × 14" wire being inserted into the base of a carnation calyx.

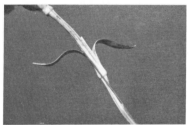

2. The wire has been wound around the stem and now acts as a support.

3. Point of insertion when wiring a rose.

4 Point of insertion when wiring an iris.

5. Point of insertion when wiring a tulip.

TRIANGULAR ARRANGEMENT

Ingredients
12 blue iris
10 Pink Chiffon roses
12 Red Copeland tulips
14 sprigs of pittosporum

1. Using a plastic bowl filled with 'Oasis' 5 iris constitute the initial stages of the outline.

2. 2 roses 4 iris and 1 tulip have been added to further substantiate the line.

3. 2 roses and 4 tulips finalize the outline. Note depth given by projecting some flowers over the container front.

4. 5 roses and 3 tulips commence the filling-in process working from the edges towards the centre.

5. 1 rose, 4 tulips and 3 iris are the final flower ingredient to be incorporated.

6. 14 sprigs of pittosporum have been used to fill up any gaps and complete the arrangement.

ALL-THE-WAY-ROUND ARRANGEMENT

Ingredients
33 freesia

11 daffodils
18 sprigs of pittosporum

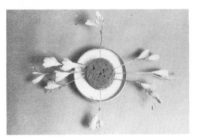

1. Using an 'Oasis' container 8 freesia provide the four salient points of the outline.

2. Another 7 freesia complete the horizontal outline. 1 freesia, centrally placed, governs the height of the arrangement.

3. 8 freesia commence filling-in the arrangement. A gradation takes place between the central high point and the perimeter flowers.

4. Another 9 freesia have been incorporated and further substantiate the filling-in process.

5. 11 daffodils complete the flower ingredient and give substance to the decoration.

6. 18 small sprigs of pittosporum fill up any remaining gaps.

ASYMMETRICAL ARRANGEMENT

Ingredients
18 muscari   1 stem A.Y.R. spray
4 freesia   chrysanthemum

1. Using a small urn 6 muscari provide the top and bottom outline points.

2. 4 more muscari substantiate the two extremities and a further 2 establish the width.

3. The remaining 6 muscari complete the asymmetrical outline.

4. 4 stems of freesia commence to fill-in the main body of the arrangement.

5. The 5 flowers and buds from 1 stem of A.Y.R. spray chrysanthemum continue the filling-in.

6. 3 chrysanthemum leaves finish off a charming petite arrangement.

ALL-THE-WAY-ROUND ARRANGEMENT

Ingredients
16 hyacinths

11 small pieces eucalyptus foliage (say ½ bunch)

1. 4 hyacinths establish the length. A pinholder has been used because hyacinth stems are too soft for 'Oasis'.

2. 4 more hyacinths continue the outline one of which establishes the height.

3. Another 4 hyacinths fill in the centre part of the decoration.

4. The last 4 hyacinths fill in the centre part of the decoration.

5. 11 pieces of eucalyptus foliage help to lighten and also complete the arrangement.

Spring is the time for bulb flowers, and flower arranging would be very dull without the tremendous range of tulips and daffodils. The most versatile, however, is undoubtedly the hyacinth. An attractive colour range, a superb perfume, suitable as a cut flower, it is as a potted plant that the hyacinth reigns supreme.

Available from before Christmas until April hyacinths are easy to grow and inexpensive to buy in pots. The bulbs are only grown in Holland and thanks must be given once again to the Dutch for their skill and patience.

L-SHAPED ARRANGEMENT

Ingredients
15 pieces of lilac (about 1 bunch)
14 tulips

1. Using a rectangular basket 5 pieces of lilac provide the 'L' shape.

2. 6 tulips substantiate the salient points.

3. 4 pieces of lilac commence to unite the vertical and horizontal extremities.

4. 5 tulips have been incorporated as part of the filling-in process.

5. 3 more tulips together with 3 pieces of lilac nearly complete this L-shaped arrangement.

6. 3 pieces of lilac and 2 pieces of lilac foliage fill in the remaining gaps to complete.

TRIANGULAR ARRANGEMENT

Ingredients
18 white carnations
13 pieces of mimosa (say 1 bunch)

1. A pottery trough with a block of 'Oasis' has 5 carnations establishing the three corners of the triangle.

2. 6 more carnations complete the triangular outline.

3. The remaining 7 carnations have been used to fill in the centre part of the triangle.

4. 13 pieces of mimosa have been incorporated to fill up any gaps that remain.

This series of small books i.e. "Spring", "Summer", "Autumn" and "Winter" Flower Arranging are essentially instructional and endeavour to convey the basic techniques involved.

The arrangements are based on geometric designs and the assembly procedures for the many different easy-to-get seasonal flowers are detailed. The basic shapes however lend themselves to considerable elaboration and the ingredients can become more varied and sophisticated.

Having mastered the assembly techniques the keen flower arranger will look further afield, so as to become more competent and experienced.

There is no better way to proficiency than to build up a library of flower arrangement books. Fortunately there is a fascinating bibliography dealing with the world's most popular indoor pastime, but it is not possible here to give an exhaustive list of the many talented authors worth reading. However, the following have written and illustrated books which have become justifiable best-sellers and can be categorised as "master" flower decorators.

Julia Clements, Stella Coe, Dodds Beb, Joy Fleming, Sheila MacQueen, Betty Massingham, Pulbrook and Gould, Violet Stevenson and, last but by no means least, Constance Spry.

CRESCENT ARRANGEMENT

Ingredients
21 double tulips

10 small pieces of eucalyptus (say ½ bunch)

1. 6 tulips provide the Crescent extremities in a handled rectangular basket containing a block of 'Oasis'.

2. 3 tulips establish the central point and a further 2 tulips commence forming the outer edge.

3. 5 tulips complete the outlines of the Crescent.

4. The remaining 5 tulips fill up the central area leaving the arrangement substantially complete.

5. 10 pieces of eucalyptus foliage have been used to mask any gaps.

Occasionally it is either necessary or desirable to wire tulips and certain other flowers before incorporating them into the arrangement. Details of this technique are given, with step-by-step pictures, in the first section of this book. The great advantage of a wired flower is that the stem can be bent in any direction and this position held. Ramrod stiff or alternatively limp and bowed tulips can be disciplined. Wiring takes practise if it is to be done properly and neatly — but it is well worth persevering as it will add to your versatility.

TRIANGULAR ARRANGEMENT

Ingredients
**27 stems of lily-of-the-valley
with natural leaves**

1. A small block of 'Oasis' has been placed into the top segment of a posy ring.

2. 8 lily-of-the-valley leaves form a triangular outline.

3. 14 flower stems have been added to the outline and appear to be growing naturally.

4. 7 lily-of-the-valley flower stems commence to fill in the centre of the decoration.

5. The final 6 flower stems complete the filling-in procedure and the arrangement.

Lily-of-the-valley is available all the year round and the tubers come all the way from Hamburg. It is forced under glass by specialist growers for use by skilled florists in wedding bouquets. In the late Spring however, Lily-of-the-valley, protected in cold frames or from the open ground, becomes available at very reasonable prices and this is the time to make use of this beautiful flower with its delicate florets and fragrant perfume.

ASYMMETRICAL ARRANGEMENT

1. 4 wallflowers establish the arrangement curves in an elegant copper jug.

2. 4 more wallflowers commence building the curving lines.

3. The top and bottom curves have nearly been joined by using a further 6 wallflowers.

4. 5 wallflowers have been added and complete the Hogarth curve.

5. The arrangement has been consolidated by inserting the final 5 wallflowers.

During the Spring there are a large selection of flowering pot plants available. Hyacinths, daffodils and tulips all make colourful pot plants and are very good either on their own or incorporated into miniature gardens or mixed planted bowls. Cinerarias are excellent value. Red, pink and cream poinsettias are becoming increasingly available outside the immediate Christmas period. Chrysanthemum pots are always a colourful stand-by for the dreary corner which needs brightening. Cyclamen (particularly Silver Sovereign) are readily available and excellent value.

DIAGONAL ARRANGEMENT

Ingredients
9 pieces palm (say 1 bunch)
12 Alladin tulips

7 small sprigs of box foliage

1. In a dish with a block of 'Oasis' 9 pieces of palm (pussy willow) provide the basic line.

2. 4 tulips have been worked into the diagonal line.

3. 3 more tulips have been incorporated and further substantiate the line.

4. The remaining 5 tulips complete the arrangement except for finishing touches.

5. 7 small sprigs of box foliage mask the 'Oasis' and give depth.

For over 400 years the Dutch have been hybridising tulips and extending the fascinating range of colours and shapes. When using tulips in flower decorations it is most important to make sure that they are taking water up the stems, otherwise they will become limp.

Cut ½" off the bottom of the stems, roll in newspaper and plunge the tulips up to their necks in cold water for at least 1 hour before arranging. Keep the tulips out of direct sunlight and draughts. If possible put the arrangement in a cool airy location.

L-SHAPED ARRANGEMENT

Ingredients
9 double stock

12 white irises
12 sprigs of larch foliage

1. In a bowl with 'Oasis' 2 stems of stock and 2 irises establish the top and bottom sectors.

2. 2 stock and 4 iris have been used to build inwards to the central corner.

3. 5 stock complete the central outline. Note how No. 5 projects over the front of the bowl.

4. 6 iris complete the flower ingredient and accentuate the L-shaped angle.

5. 12 sprigs of larch put the final touches and help to lighten the decoration.

Steeped in the mists of antiquity lies the origin of Mothering Sunday – the big day when mothers are particularly honoured by their children. The festival is fixed in the Church Calendar as the third Sunday before Easter and consequently varies in date. Depending upon circumstances flowers are plentiful or otherwise – and flowers are the only real gift for this occasion. Most flower growers grow extra for the Mother's Day festival so as to keep prices down. Many florists work on tiny margins to allow the children's pocket money to go further.

TRIANGULAR ARRANGEMENT

Ingredients
8 yellow iris
20 Actaea narcissi

14 pieces of grevillea (say 1 bunch)
6 double freesia

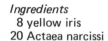

1. In an 'Oasis' container 4 iris, 5 narcissi and 8 pieces of grevillea establish the outline.

2. 4 iris and 3 narcissi commence the filling-in process. Note how 4, 5, 6 and 7 project horizontally.

3. 5 narcissi and 6 double freesia have been added as substance to the main body.

4. 6 narcissi have been worked into the central part of the arrangement.

5. 6 pieces of grevillea and remaining narcissi fill up the gaps and complete the faced arrangement.

On rare occasions a world beating 'sport' appears amongst a mundane crop of flowers and the fortunate grower suddenly finds that he has a winner. A few years ago a double flowered freesia was discovered and, after several seasons of patient corm propagation, it has now become available to flower arrangers. Powerfully scented, the double freesia is limited to white cream and lavender at the moment and it only flowers in the mid-Spring months. It is, however, a particularly welcome addition to the ever increasing range of flowers now available.

ALL-THE-WAY-ROUND ARRANGEMENT

Ingredients
42 polyanthus
12 polyanthus leaves

1. In a bowl with crumpled 2" wire netting 12 polyanthus establish the outline and 3 polyanthus the height.

2. 9 polyanthus commence the process of building up the arrangement from the circumference towards the centre.

3. 9 more polyanthus continue the filling-in and building up.

4. The remaining 9 polyanthus complete the flower content and the arrangement appears rather 'heavy' at this stage.

5. 12 polyanthus leaves added at random break up and lighten the final appearance.

It is important to make sure that there are no airlocks or blocked capillaries in the stem otherwise water will not flow and the flower will die prematurely. Soft stemmed flowers should have ½" removed with a sharp knife or scissors from the bottom of the stem using an oblique cut.

Woody stemmed flowers such as chrysanthemums, lilac etc. should have the bottom 2" of the stem crushed with a hammer or split with a knife. In the latter case the scraping off of the outside bark will also be helpful.

CRESCENT ARRANGEMENT

Ingredients
12 Parrot tulips

43 sprigs of broom
(say 1 bunch)

1. 8 sprigs of broom establish the extremities of the Crescent in a boat-shaped basket with 'Oasis'.

2. 3 more broom sprigs and 4 tulips consolidate the extremities.

3. 5 broom sprigs and 3 tulips complete the outline.

4. 5 tulips have been used to fill up the central part (focal point) of the arrangement.

5. 15 sprigs of broom have been incorporated in the process of lightening and gap-filling.

6. 12 remaining broom sprigs complete an arrangement with an unusual and elegant line.

DIAGONAL ARRANGEMENT

Ingredients
21 stems lily-of-the-valley
6 bluebells

3 carnations
6 sprigs of lilac foliage

1. In a round basket filled with 'Oasis' 4 stems of lily-of-the-valley and 2 bluebells establish the extremities.

2. 2 valley and 4 bluebells commence the link-up of the upper and lower extremities.

3. 15 stems of valley complete the diagonal outline.

4. 3 carnations provide focal interest. The central carnation is recessed to give depth to the arrangement.

5. 6 sprigs of lilac foliage have been added at random to hide 'Oasis' and fill any gaps.

Flowers are used to grace all the great occasions and it is, perhaps, at the wedding when the skill of the florist comes particularly to the forefront.

The British method of bouquet making is much more delicate and intricate than the techniques used on the Continent and in America. Very many tiny florets are each individually wired and carefully assembled into the bouquet. This skilful painstaking task, ensuring a beautiful neat bouquet of quality, seems to be lacking when the Continental method is adopted and complete stems of flowers are incorporated.

TRIANGULAR ARRANGEMENT

Ingredients
20 Semper Avanti narcissi
15 small pieces of larch

1. In an 'Oasis' container 4 narcissi commence the outline.

2. 5 more narcissi complete the outline of the "right-angled" triangle (as opposed to the more common "isosceles").

3. 11 narcissi have been incorporated and fill-up the main body of the decoration. No. 9 has been recessed.

4. 5 pieces of larch commence the final filling-in of any gaps.

5. 10 more pieces of larch complete the arrangement. Several narcissi are in bud to last well.

Spring is the time to watch the baby buds burgeon forth. Pussy willow is particularly good value in this respect. Starting off with the grey furry catkins, they soon turn yellow — to be followed by the tiny green leaves. As a cut foliage the salixes are terribly good value.

Horse chestnut, known as 'sticky bud' will slowly but surely develop in water and eventually unfold their exciting fresh green leaves.

Be careful, however, of some of the very young foliages. Many tend to be extremely soft and will not last well.

LINE ARRANGEMENT *(see cover)*

Ingredients

9 stems of forsythia   9 daffodils
6 yellow iris   11 polyanthus leaves

1. 9 stems of forsythia provide a basic outline using a square dish with 'Oasis'.

2. 3 iris commence substantiating the downward line.

3. 3 more iris complete the line of the arrangement.

4. 9 daffodils add further interest to the arrangement. Being in bud they will last well.

5. 11 polyanthus leaves give depth to the lower part of the decoration and mask the 'Oasis'.

This book is one of a quartet which demonstrate the techniques required when assembling flower arrangements. All the easy-to-get flowers during the four seasons of the year have been used on one or more occasion. Having mastered the methods contained in these books it would be natural to seek further fields to conquer.

In "Party Flower Arranging", "Church Flower Arranging", and "Christmas Flower Arranging" (all these books are already or will soon be available) many charming and sophisticated arrangements are portrayed and detailed — providing new ideas and advanced techniques.